IMAGES
of America

CONCORD

MASSACHUSETTS

Lulu (Louisa) Nieriker, Louisa May Alcott's niece, came to America after her mother, May Alcott Nieriker, died of complications following the birth. Louisa raised Lulu at her sister's request. When Louisa died, Lulu returned to Europe to live with her father. She married Emil Rasim and made her home in Switzerland. She died in 1976.

IMAGES
of America

CONCORD
MASSACHUSETTS

Sarah Chapin

ARCADIA
PUBLISHING

Published by Arcadia Publishing
Charleston, South Carolina

For all general information contact Arcadia Publishing at:
Telephone 843-853-2070
Fax 843-853-0044
E-Mail sales@arcadiapublishing.com
For customer service and orders:
Toll-Free 1-888-313-2665

Visit us on the Internet at www.arcadiapublishing.com

Egg Rock is the site of the confluence of the Sudbury and Assabet Rivers, forming the Concord River. The plaque says: "On the hill Nashawtuck at the meeting of the rivers and along the banks lived the Indian owners of Musketaquid before the white men came."

Contents

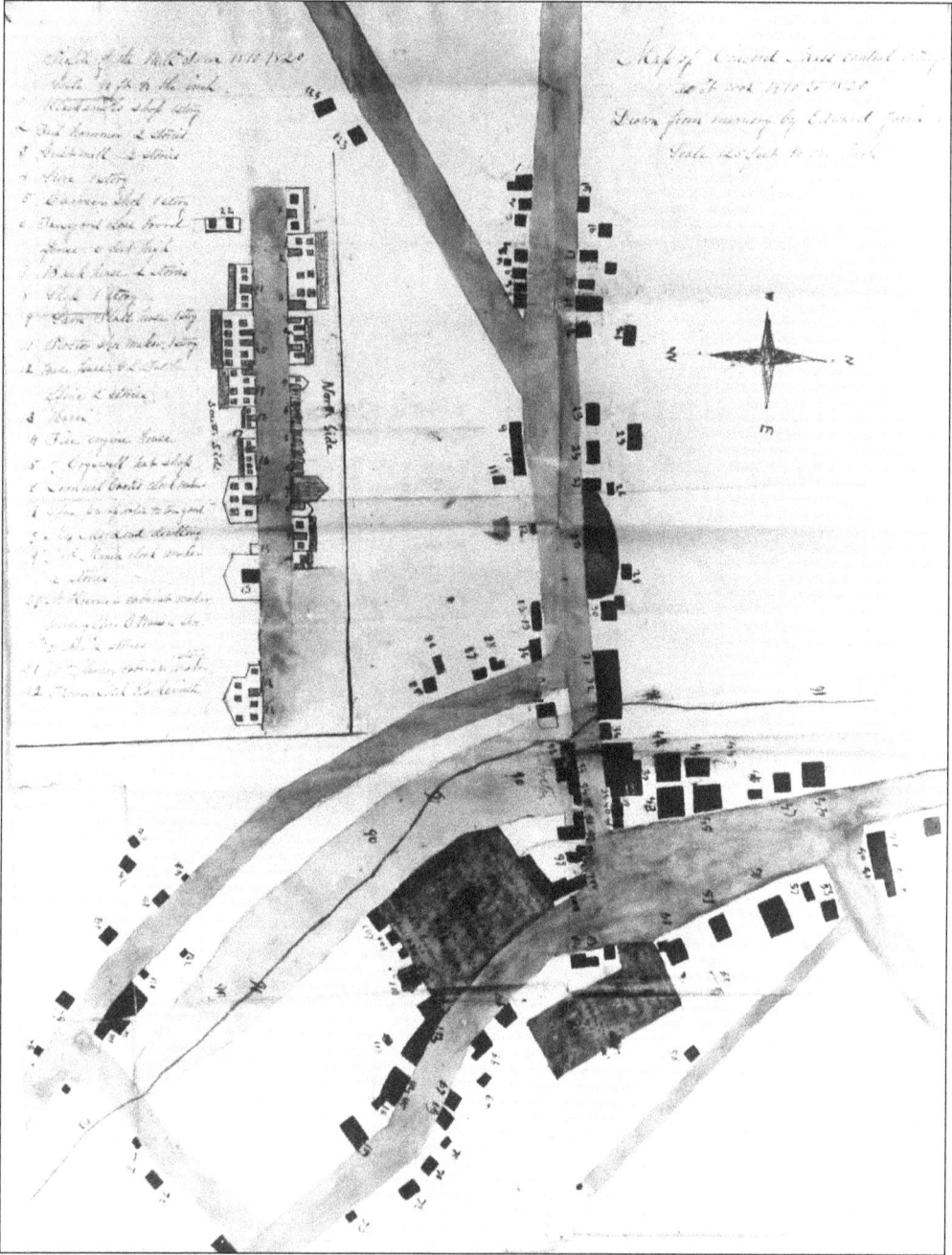

Edward Jarvis's map of Concord Center was drawn from memory in 1883. It supplements his historical volume, *Houses and People*. Jarvis grew up on the Milldam and enjoyed wandering about the shops and watching the men work. He was particularly intrigued by the mechanism of the waterwheel.

Introduction

How Concord Lives With Its Historic Past

Concord has always been special. Two reasons deriving from the beginning of the town's existence may be cited. First, it was the only settlement out of range of the ocean. That meant the necessity for an enterprising spirit to endure the rigors of wilderness living. Second, the Rev. Peter Bulkeley and Capt. Simon Willard (to whom the land grant was given by the Massachusetts Bay General Court on September 2, 1635) brought no previously gathered assemblage with them. The twelve settling families came from quite different places in England to join in the creation of the new township. Rev. Bulkeley named his community *concord*: amicable union. It was to be a place of freedom from "oppression, griping, and hard dealing" where men and women could "walk in peace, love, mercy and equity toward each other."[1]

Concord was 140 years old when the group of militant colonists marched across the North Bridge to confront advancing British soldiers in the first skirmish of the Revolutionary War. That event was "the hinge . . . on which the large revolving future was to turn,"[2] to make Concord a community symbolic of political freedom all over the world.

The men and women who established Concord's social and legal standards of decency and constancy endowed the community with gentility, restraint, and good old-fashioned New England grit. That sense of historic accountability, stamped into their seventh generation sons' and daughters' genes, explains why Henry James called the town "the biggest little place in America."[3] It is not inconsistent with its political past, therefore, that Concord became the home of the Titans of mid-nineteenth century literature and philosophy: Bronson and Louisa May Alcott, Henry David Thoreau, Ralph Waldo Emerson, Nathaniel Hawthorne, and William Ellery Channing; and the home of others perhaps less well known: William Munroe (whose invention of the lead pencil may have been the first in America), Ephraim Wales Bull (who developed a new species of purple grape named for the town), and Harrison Gray Dyar (who, some say, invented the first telegraphy device and successfully tested it on the Lowell Road).

The invention of photography in 1839 contributed to the successful management of this momentous legacy. It gave Concord's historic past potential contemporary presence. Many venerable ancestors, who were known previously only through their journals, letters, books, drawings, and paintings, suddenly had faces. Historic sites, at the mercy of weather and the necessities of modern living, were no longer overlooked.

Throughout their history, Concordians have formed clubs, lawn parties, river parties, dances, theatrical troupes, musical organizations, athletic associations, social groups, philanthropic and fraternal societies, church endeavors, and celebrations for family affairs and town holidays. Not all important landmarks have survived time's vicissitudes, and some are not recognizable to today's citizens. The center of town has actually changed relatively little, yet farmland has practically disappeared from the outlying landscape. Treasured vistas have been shorn and shrunk by community developers whose economic perspective has differed from the sentiments of citizens to whom open space is a gift. In the 1930s, construction of the Concord bypass destroyed precious wild flower sites; the trade-off was that the center of town received less traffic. Old roads, as well as newly laid-out streets on former farmland, have required sluices, culverts, and causeways. Concord's bridges, all of which have figured in the town's historic development, have had to be renovated, widened, and reassessed to accommodate modern vehicles. The North Bridge, vulnerable to destruction from spring freshets, has been reconstructed four times: in 1874, 1889, 1909, and 1956. Floods, hurricanes, and ice storms, endured heroically, have been dramatically recorded.

Concord has been fortunate in the refinement and skill of its photographic artists. Alfred Winslow Hosmer (1851–1903), a native Concordian, made portraits as keepsakes for local residents and landscape photographs for sale to tourists who came to visit Walden Pond and the North Bridge. The Library owns 680 glass-plate images made by Hosmer mainly during the 1880s and 1890s. The work of other photographers inspired by the remarkable heritage and charm of the Concord area—Herbert W. Gleason (1855–1937), Alfred Munroe (1817–1904), Henry Allen Castle (1869–1962), and Frederick Alonzo Tower (1871–1959)—is represented in the Concord Library photograph collection as well.

This collection of Concord photographs informs memory and endorses imagination. The images confirm that the town has maintained its historic legacy with grace, determination, and wit. The parson from Bedfordshire and the fur-trader from Kent would be gratified.

1. Townsend Scudder, *Concord: American Town* (Boston: Little, Brown and Company, 1947), 12.
2. Henry James, *The American Scene* (New York: Harper & Brothers, 1907), 251.
3. Ibid., 247

Acknowledgments

All the images in this publication are the property of the Concord Free Public Library and are printed here with permission. I would like to thank the President of the Library Trustees, Annabelle W. Shepherd; Library Director Barbara Powell; Special Collections Curator Leslie Perrin Wilson; and Staff Assistant Joyce Woodman for assistance, encouragement, and forbearance. Special thanks to Marcia Moss for editorial guidance.

One

Concord People

Bronson Alcott (1799–1888) is photographed here with Louisa in 1885 in front of the School of Philosophy next to Orchard House, the Alcott family home. Ellen Emerson is in the rear buggy. This may be the last picture of Bronson Alcott. It is from a glass plate in the Allen French Collection.

Mary Moody Emerson (1774–1863) was the daughter of Ralph Waldo Emerson's grandfather. An unconventional woman in all respects (she was just over four feet tall), she nevertheless exerted a strong influence on her nephews. Regularly brusque, impatient beyond civility, she was capable of tenderness when it pleased her to express it.

Squire Samuel Hoar (1778–1856), Ralph Waldo Emerson said admiringly, "was born under a Christian and human star, full of mansuetude and nobleness, honor and charity: and whilst he dared to do all that might be seen by man, his self respect restrained him from any foolhardiness."

The Reverend Ezra Ripley (1751–1841) was elected to the ministry May 11, 1778, seven days before Squire Samuel Hoar was born. He retired in 1840. He guided the parish into an era of steadily increasing religious freedom, surviving the departure from his congregation of a group of more conservative Trinitarians.

The jailer made famous for keeping Thoreau in jail in 1846, Sam Staples (1813–1895), also served as a representative in the state legislature. He was a selectman, superintendent of public grounds, auctioneer, and a trustee of the Middlesex Institution for Savings. His shrewd business sense and ribald wit made him a favorite town figure.

11

Edward Jarvis (1803–1884) is remembered as an historian, a statistician, and an advocate for humane care of the mentally ill. His memoir, *Traditions and Reminiscences of Concord*, is a fascinating record of life in the community from the end of the Revolutionary War to the middle of the nineteenth century.

Dr. Josiah Bartlett (1796–1878) was the leading physician in Concord until his death in 1878. He was considered to be the quintessential country doctor, despite a quick temper and a strong belief in the evil of strong drink. He was president of both the Middlesex Medical Society (1858) and the Massachusetts Medical Society (1862).

The Emerson family lived in the house they called "Bush," located at the junction of the Cambridge Turnpike and the Bay (Lexington) Road. Here pictured are Lidian and Ralph Waldo Emerson with their children, Ellen, Edith, and Edward, and their grandchildren.

Elizabeth Palmer Peabody, sister of Sophia Hawthorne and Mary Mann, is seen here with Mr. and Mrs. Lothrop and Margaret. Elizabeth Peabody was an associate in Bronson Alcott's Temple School in Boston, but later opposed his educational theories. She continued her friendship with the family, however, and often visited them when she was in Concord.

Nathaniel Hawthorne (1804–1864), called New England's Chaucer by Ellery Channing, was the first non-minister to live in the Old Manse. Melancholia colored his life as well as that of his children, but his dark genius notwithstanding, his stories still catch the public's imagination after one hundred twenty-five years.

The Maxham portrait of Henry David Thoreau (1856) is one of three extant images of Concord's famous poet-naturalist. This view, made by Alfred Hosmer from the original, shows Thoreau at age thirty-nine, before he became seriously ill. Thoreau died on Main Street in 1862, and is buried in Sleepy Hollow Cemetery.

Amos Bronson Alcott, a friend to all Concord's resident transcendentalists, was a neoplatonist (his vision was compatible with both Emerson's and Thoreau's principles), and his views were well received especially in the western United States during the mid-1800s.

Ralph Waldo Emerson is Concord's most famous poet and philosopher. He bore great losses, he gave generously, materially and intellectually, to friends and neighbors, and throughout he wrote with perceptive depth and clarity. Emerson suffered from a senile aphasia as he grew older, and his communicative genius was silenced before his death in 1882.

Ellery Channing (1817–1901) was a poet with a personality to match his art. He was by turns charming and cruel, humorous and melancholic. His marriage to Margaret Fuller's sister Ellen was disastrous, but his genuine friendships with Thoreau and Emerson give posterity an opportunity to appreciate this conflicted man.

Abba May Alcott (1800–1877) was a woman of great stamina and patience. She loved her husband and her daughters, and she bore their rigors of poverty with fortitude and fierce pride. A letter from Mrs. Alcott to Mrs. Thoreau at the time of Henry's illness expresses sorrow at the approaching "inevitable bereavement."

Lidian Emerson, seen here with her grandchildren, was Ralph Waldo Emerson's second wife. She lived in the shadow of her famous husband (at considerable emotional cost to herself), yet was a loyal wife and mother. Her friendship with Thoreau sustained them both while Emerson lectured away from Concord. Lidian died in 1892.

Louisa May Alcott (1832–1888), the second Alcott daughter, devoted her life to writing in order to support the family. She served as a nurse during the Civil War, contracted typhoid fever, and suffered from ill health thereafter. In spite of her infirmities, she was an eloquent spokeswoman for women's rights. Alcott is shown here with the actor James Edward Murdoch (1811-1893).

Daniel Chester French (1850–1931), Concord's most distinguished sculptor, created the Minuteman statue (partly from pieces of old cannon). Other famous works include the Lincoln Memorial in Washington, John Harvard, and the memorial statue for the Melvin family, in Concord, considered to be his finest outdoor work.

Ellen Emerson (1839–1909), the first daughter born to Ralph Waldo and Lidian (Jackson) Emerson, was named for her father's first wife, Ellen Tucker. Ellen's biographical essay about her mother shows Ellen's literary skill, sympathy, and understanding. She is seen here standing behind the donkey, Graciosa.

Frederick Pratt (1863–1910), the first son of Anna and John Pratt, nephew of Louisa May Alcott, and grandson of horticulturist Minot Pratt, enjoyed tinkering with automobiles and bicycles. His frail constitution is reflected in his last words as he retired to bed (where he died unexpectedly); he said, "I have lost half a pound today."

The Concord Home for the Aged was started by the Concord Female Charitable Society (the men called it the "chattable" society) as a home for ladies, but Martha Hunt donated $20,000 to the Home in memory of her father, stipulating that it should thereupon serve men as well as women. It was incorporated in 1887.

Phoebe Foster (1797–1886) lived on Lexington Road near the church. She was a recipient of the town's generous program of charitable care, yet "always bawling for more," according to John Keyes. In her ninetieth year, all nursing care, board for the nurse, medications, and burial were paid by the Overseers of the Poor.

Edward Waldo Emerson (1844–1930) married Annie Keyes in 1874. He became a doctor to please his father, but gave up his medical practice in 1882, after his father died. His second career in art and writing gave this gentle man great satisfaction. A devoted horseman, Edward continued to ride until he was 82.

Ephraim Wales Bull (1806–1895), originally a goldsmith apprenticed to Louis Lauriat in Boston, came to Concord in August 1836. He continued in that trade until he was in his late sixties. He began cultivating grapes in the 1840s. The first Concord Grape was marketed in 1854.

Alfred Munroe (1817–1904) was born in Concord. He died in Concord after being struck by a horse and carriage at the junction of Sudbury and Main Streets. His photography is representative of his wise judgment, gentle and perceptive love of nature, and his affection for the town of his birth.

George Bartlett, pictured on the right, received a congratulatory letter from Edward Jarvis about his *Concord Guide Book*. Jarvis said, "It is an interesting book . . . you have been very successful in your historical inquiries, and successful in your presentation of your stores of local knowledge." It was high praise from the crusty old historian.

Franklin Sanborn, private schoolteacher, editor of the *Springfield Republican*, social activist, abolitionist, founder of the National Prison Association, and biographer, had both energy and wit. His biography of Thoreau in 1882 has not survived without criticism.

George Frisbie Hoar was born in Concord in 1826. He was elected to Congress in 1868 and to the Senate in 1877, where he remained until 1900. Frisbie, as he was known, wrote a two-volume autobiography filled with anecdotes and reminiscences of his youth in Concord and his professional life in Washington D.C.

Elizabeth Hoar (1814–1878) was the oldest of the children born to Samuel and Sarah (Sherman) Hoar. She was engaged to Charles Emerson (Ralph Waldo Emerson's brother), but he died just before the wedding date. Aunt Lizzie, as she was called, remained close to the Emerson family.

Harvey Wheeler (1847–1917) was a prominent Concord manufacturer, who gave generously in time and energy to the town, but never lost his ability to relate to his employees. He operated the Boston Harness Company after 1891 and became president of the Middlesex Institution for Savings in 1900.

The Concord Artillery, incorporated in 1804, received an emotional send-off on April 19, 1861. Dressed in their Napoleonic uniforms, they raised the flag (on a staff cut from a tree near Walden Pond) after a speech by Judge Hoar and a prayer by Rev. Grindall Reynolds, and, surrounded by their families, marched to the depot. When the war was over and the men returned to Concord, the judge "stood" before them and called up one and another by name, with a word or two of praise and affection: "Captain Humphrey Buttrick, we are proud of you, son of that honored name!"

Capt. Daniel Tuttle's wife, Emeline, had thirteen children. She is famous for saying (when her husband was called to defend Washington during the Civil War), "Go. We will get along someway." She managed the large farm and the children by herself until Capt. Tuttle returned. She died in 1904, aged 88.

Spanish-American recruits were ordered to prepare for war with Spain in the spring of 1898. Concord voted that no married men should be allowed to enter active service, but some exceptions were made. Edward Waldo Emerson headed the War Committee and made a farewell speech. The boulder on Monument Square facing the Colonial Inn is a memorial to the men lost in that campaign.

Alfred Winslow Hosmer, an ardent admirer of Thoreau, photographed many important sites referred to by Thoreau in his *Journal*. Books belonging to Thoreau and letters from Thoreau's friends, which Hosmer collected and preserved, were given to the Concord Library by his nephew. He died of a massive stroke during a thunderstorm in 1903.

Ebenezer Rockwood Hoar (1816–1895) graduated from Harvard in 1835. Among others in the class were Richard Henry Dana and H.G.O. Blake, Thoreau's executor. Judge Hoar served in Congress and as attorney general of the United States. He was President Grant's host in 1875 when Grant attended the centennial celebration.

Ruth Robinson Wheeler (1890–1973) was one of Concord's most eminent historians. She worked for the Minutemen National Park and the *Concord Journal* and belonged to the Antiquarian Society. Her book, *Climate for Freedom*, published in 1967, is a standard reference work for anyone conducting research in Concord's historic past.

Charles Hosmer Walcott (1848–1901) began as a storekeeper in Concord Center, but his real career was as a lawyer-historian. His *Concord in the Colonial Period* (1884) is a model of well-documented scholarship. He served the town as superintendent of schools and also as chairman of the Board of Assessors.

Lemuel Shattuck (1793–1859) described the beginning years of the town and its growth into a thriving community in his *History of Concord* (1835). This remarkable man was a founder of the New England Historic Genealogical Society and the American Statistical Society. He lived in Concord from 1823 until 1834.

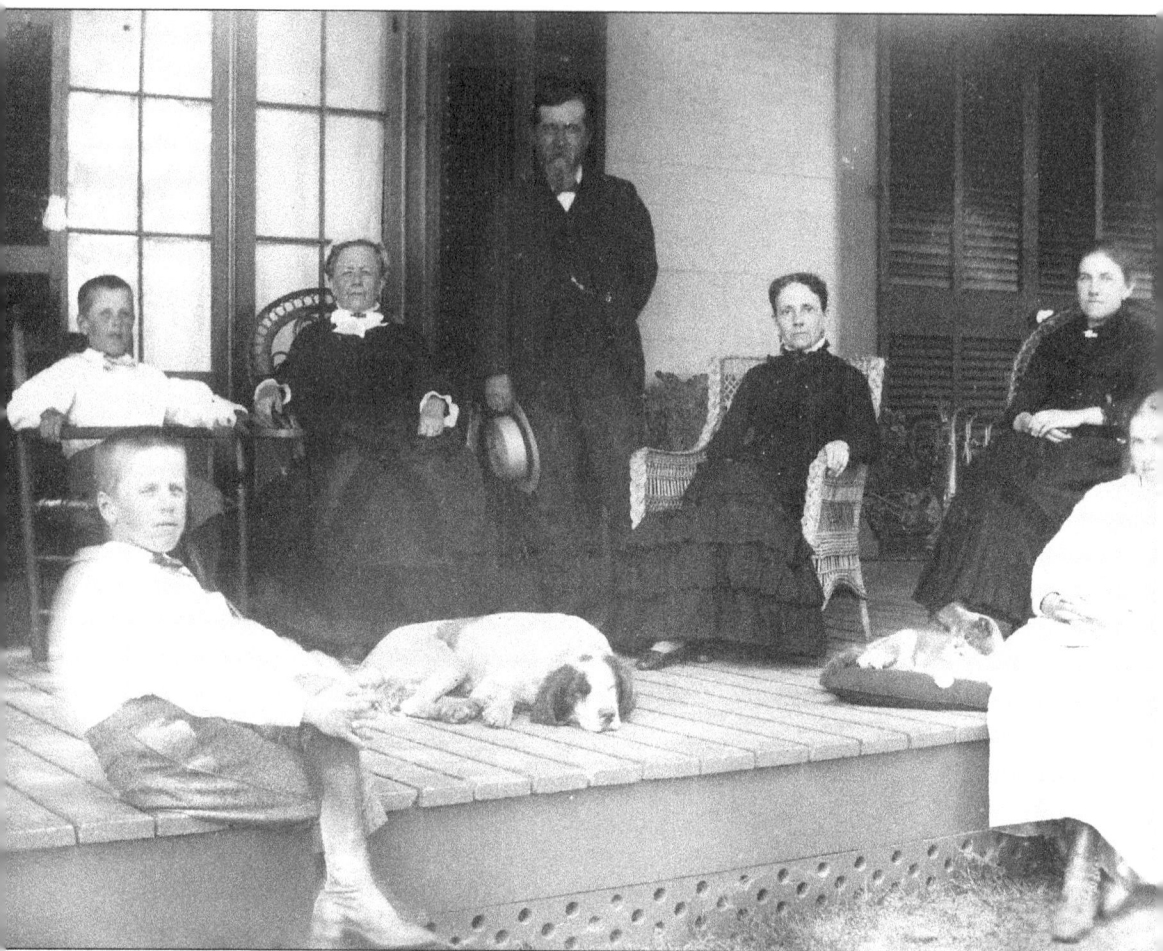

John Shepard Keyes (1821–1910) lived at the time of the great change in Concord from an agrarian to a mercantile economy. During his long life, he participated in every important event in the town, including the laying out of Sleepy Hollow Cemetery and the centennial celebration in 1875. He was solidly built, "with keen eyes, a rather ruddy face, and the moustache, side whiskers, and full beard of his day and generation. . . . His frankness was at times almost startling, as, in commenting on the death of a fellow townsman, he said ' "Blank" died last night, some us pleased and everybody satisfied.' "

George Merrick Brooks (1824–1893) gave up his career in the United States Congress because Washington's torrid climate disagreed with him. He preferred being the Judge of Probate for Middlesex County. Frisbie Hoar said of him, "I think George Brooks's smile would be enough to console any widow in an ordinary affliction."

Thomas Whitney Surette (1861–1941) grew up on Lexington Road where the informal musical gatherings in his childhood inspired him later to form the famous Concord School of Music, a summer school for amateur music performers and teachers. Surette's *Concord Series* is still used by teachers and chorus conductors.

Lawyer Nathan Brooks (1785–1863) was born in Lincoln. His adult years were spent in Concord, where he held positions in the bank, Middlesex Mutual Fire Insurance Company, Congregational Ministerial Fund, Trustees of Town Donations, and the Middlesex Agricultural Society. He was a temperate man, patient, wise, humorous, and scrupulously honest.

Hapgood Wright (1811–1896) was one of Concord's most generous benefactors. He left money for the town forest now called Fairyland, a gift to Emerson Hospital, and long-term bequests of current significance to the town. It amused him to hand out five-dollar bills with his picture in place of Lincoln's image.

Sarah Alden Bradford Ripley (1793–1867), a youthful protégé of Mary Moody Emerson (the eccentric aunt of Ralph Waldo Emerson), was a woman of simplicity and kindliness, but she is best remembered as a classical scholar and teacher. She and her husband, Samuel Ripley, lived at the Old Manse in their later years.

Alicia Keyes (1855–1924), the daughter of John and Martha Keyes, studied art with Mary Wheeler and May Alcott. During the winter of 1862, she lived with the Emerson family, and from 1884–87, she traveled abroad for reasons of health. She counted John Singer Sargent and Isabella Stewart Gardner among her friends.

Sophia Thoreau (1819–1876), the youngest of the Thoreau family, was close to her brother and was instrumental in preserving his memory through judicious responsibility for his writings. She shared his abolitionist views, his love of nature, and his perception of eternity. She was invalided early and died of tubercular peritonitis.

Two

Historic Sites

This view of the Concord Bank, incorporated in 1832, was made at the beginning of the 1880s. Former tenants using this centrally located building, besides lawyers (Nathan Brooks) and bankers (The Middlesex Institution for Savings), were a tailor and the National Express Company (seen here).

Concord Junction was one name given to the western section of Concord when, in 1872, the Old Colony Line (Framingham to Lowell)—and in 1876, a connector, the Acton, Nashua & Boston—crossed the Boston and Maine (Boston to Fitchburg) line. One hundred and twenty-five trains passed through the town daily.

In 1890, Harvey Wheeler's Harness Company was moved from the reformatory area to a site near the Derby Bridge. One hundred and twenty employees made harnesses to customer specifications and also made leather belts and holsters. A dozen families lived on the Crest Street hill in houses built by Mr. Wheeler.

The Damon Mill (seen on the far left) came into the Damon family in 1834. Material for Civil War soldiers' uniforms was manufactured on the site where, for nearly two hundred years, mills had utilized the rapid waters of the Assabet River. Edward Carver Damon (1836–1901) was the owner of the mill through the nineteenth century.

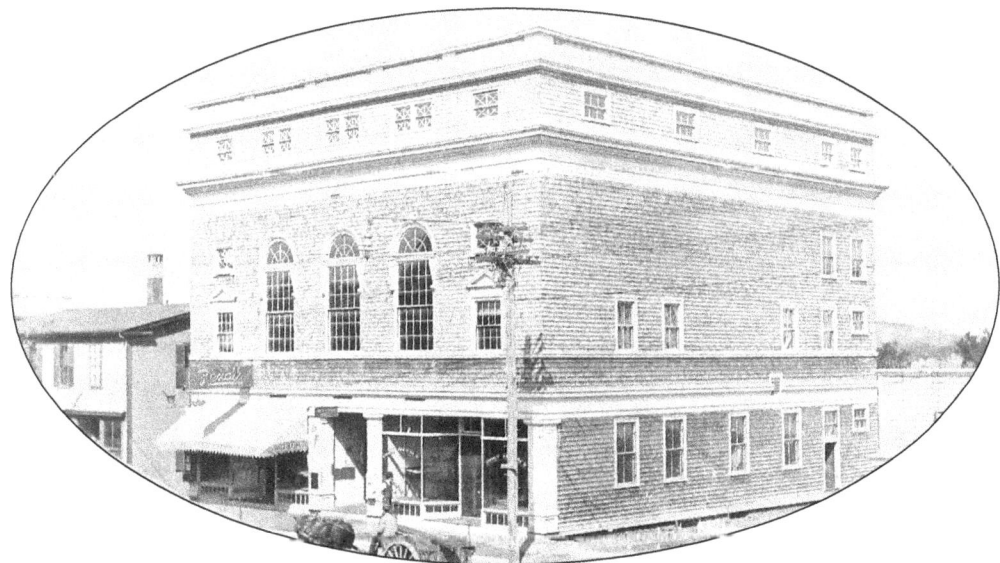

The Association Hall was above the present West Concord post office. It was on the second floor (the Odd Fellows rented the third floor) and many social events took place there. The structure was built in 1890, burned in 1903, rebuilt in 1904, and remodeled in 1935 to its present dimensions.

In the shops on the Milldam's north side, photographed one hundred years ago, you could buy leather goods, groceries, hardware, candy, shoes, and dry goods, and upstairs,

The Concord Prison, built in 1873, was opened in 1878 as a state prison with seven hundred inmates. There was dissatisfaction in Boston with the state prison so far away in Concord, so in 1884 most of the inmates were removed to Charlestown, and the prison facility became known as the Massachusetts Reformatory.

you could get your hair cut. Nowadays, you can buy clothes, hardware, lingerie, cosmetics, and herbal decorations.

The Reformatory railroad station on the Middlesex Central line was opened in 1879. Visitors to the prison could eat and spend the night in this building located to the east of the main prison, facing the Assabet River. The station house was razed when the bypass connection to the Mohawk Trail was built.

Frank Pierce's shop, built in 1828, was in what is thought to have been the oldest of the Milldam Company buildings. Mr. Pierce, known as the Dean of the Milldam, opened his store on August 31, 1865. He sold shoes to Concord's illustrious authors, and he enjoyed reporting that the Alcott girls' shoes had copper toes.

The Old Burying Ground, situated to the west of the Milldam, faced the driveway to the former Rose Hawthorne School. It was also known as Smedley's Burying Ground. The oldest stone, that of Thomas Hartshorne, is dated 1697, that is twenty years after the oldest stone in the Hill Burying Ground.

Monument Square, the center of Concord's political life, commands the east end of the Milldam. Situated around the Square are St. Bernard's Church (1868), the Town House (1851), The Insurance Company Building (early 1800s), the Colonial Inn, the Corinthian Lodge, Monument Hall, and the Catholic Rectory (antedating 1789). In the early days of the nineteenth century, during the week of the September Court, "[a]long the whole length of the Common . . . was a row of booths or board shanties erected for the sale of all sorts of drink—rum, gin, brandy etc., wine or its imitation, beer strong and weak called 'small beer.'"

The Old Manse, probably built in 1766, was remodeled in 1846 and 1875. It remained in the Ripley family from 1780 to 1939. Illustrious residents include Ralph Waldo Emerson's grandfather, Mary Moody Emerson, Nathaniel Hawthorne, and Sarah Alden Ripley. It is presently owned by the Trustees of Reservations.

John C. Friend, in his early days as a pharmacist on the Milldam, sold, besides drugs and medicine, "Pure Wines and Liquors" for medicinal purposes. Tall and distinguished, Friend was also the town treasurer until 1894 when he was replaced by one of Judge Keyes's candidates.

The Hastings house (1790) was located on the northwest corner of Walden and Main Streets. It was once the residence of the Thoreaus. John Friend tore the house down in 1892 and replaced it with a business block, which John Snow bought in 1913. On the Walden Street side was Charles Sanford's furniture store.

The Trinitarian Church on Walden Street was formed in 1826 by members of the First Parish who preferred Congregationalism to Unitarianism. The building was rebuilt in 1898 and burned in 1924. Harry Little, the Concord architect who had just completed the National Cathedral in Washington D.C., designed the present church, using granite from the railroad turnaround as foundation material.

Three houses were joined together to form the Colonial Inn. The eastern-most house, owned by the Minots, was later a residence of the Thoreaus. Thomas Surette lived in the western-most house. Armaments were stockpiled in one of the houses before the Revolutionary War began.

The small Church Green house, located next to the First Parish Church, belonged to William Munroe (1778–1861), who was an early manufacturer of lead pencils. He was the father of William, who established the Concord Free Public Library, and Alfred, one of Concord's important photographers.

The Wright Tavern (1747), originally owned by Ephraim Jones, is named for the 1775 tenant, Amos Wright. The Jarvis family lived there in the early 1800s. In 1877 it became a "temperance hotel" with stables for patrons' horses. Judge Hoar bought it in 1886 and gave it to the First Parish Church.

The Scotchford-Wheeler house may be the oldest house in town. It was built about 1653 by John Scotchford, the town clerk from 1668 to 1679. The first Wheeler to own the property was Edward, who bought it from John Scotchford in 1696. The deed has remained in the possession of family members through numerous generations.

A.B. Black's Wagon Works, established in 1875, was, by 1884, a prospering business in Concord Center. Twenty men were employed. This structure replaced his blacksmith shop destroyed by fire. A.B. Black expanded the three-story building in 1886 and again in 1890 when a fourth story was added.

By the beginning of the 1860s, Nathaniel Folsom, the high school's only teacher, told the town that his school was seriously overcrowded. In 1864 the small building was sold to Rockwood Hoar, and $10,000 was voted by the town for the construction of a new high school.

"Schoolhouse Row" on Stow Street included the new school (replaced by the Hunt Gym; it was moved to the corner of Stow and Hubbard Streets and renamed for Ezra Ripley) and

the Emerson School (1880), the first consolidated school for the younger grades, designed by John Faxon.

Ralph Waldo Emerson's House on Cambridge Turnpike was built about 1828 by Charles Coolidge, whose aunt was Thomas Jefferson's granddaughter. It was purchased by Emerson in 1835. In 1872 the house was severely damaged by a fire in the attic. It is owned now by the Emerson Memorial Association.

Connor's Well was built in 1903 for Charles Emerson (Ralph Waldo Emerson's nephew) on drained land that is now the site of Emerson Hospital and the Deaconess Home, on the Old Road to Nine Acre Corner. Either Charles Emerson or Judge Prescott Keyes put up the marker seen in the photograph.

The Hill Burying Ground's oldest stone may be Joseph Merriam's, dated 1677. Buried here are Ezra Ripley, Col. James Barrett, and Major John Buttrick, who led the Minutemen to battle at the Old North Bridge. There is also a memorial to Emerson's grandfather (the Rev. William Emerson) who died in Vermont.

The Monument Square Elm, the whipping post 1790–1820, was planted on April 19, 1776, the first anniversary of the North Bridge battle. The circular bench around it was one of Ralph

Waldo Emerson's favorite resting places. It was cut down in 1941 after suffering irreparable damage in the 1938 hurricane.

Concord's famous cemetery was designed by H.W.S. Cleveland in 1855 on land known as Sleepy Hollow, owned by Deacon Brown. The consecration was led by Mr. Emerson, and an ode by Franklin Sanborn was sung. Concord's famous authors are buried on the ridge above the hollow.

Simon Brown's River Cottage is an example of the rural architecture of the mid-nineteenth century. Brown (1802–1873) was the lieutenant governor of the state in 1853. Edward Jarvis referred to him as a "gentleman of rare intelligence, especially in all matters of agriculture and horticulture."

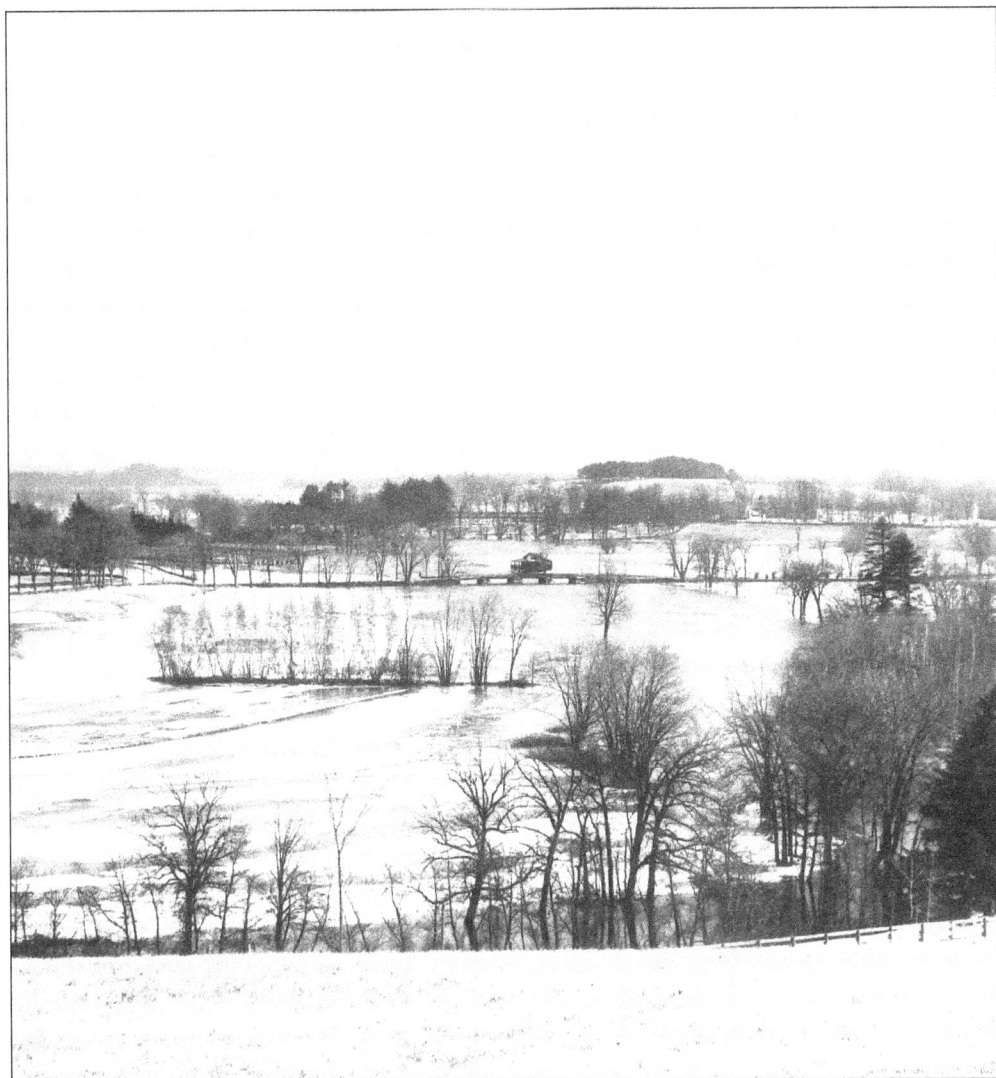

Nashawtuc Bridge, a single-arch granite block bridge, was built in 1883 by Charles Hurd, son of Isaac Hurd (proprietor of the Green Store, where the Catholic Church is now). The bridge gave access to the reservoir on top of the hill, and land from its excavation supplied fill for the causeway.

Thoreau's birthplace on Virginia Road was probably built by Deacon John Wheeler in the late 1670s. Capt. Jonas Minot owned the property at the end of the eighteenth century. Minot's second wife's daughter Cynthia married John Thoreau. Henry David Thoreau was born here in 1817. The family moved away the following year.

The interior of St. Bernard's Church on Monument Square was renovated in 1889, with architect John Chapman supervising. The dedication took place in September with officials from nearby, many clergy from neighboring towns and the Archbishop. The steeple was added at this time.

The grave of John Jack (d. 1773) is marked with an epitaph written by Daniel Bliss Jr. to celebrate Jack's freedom from slavery. It concludes, "He practiced those virtues, without which kings are but slaves." John Jack (his name was invented by Bliss) lived on Lexington Road on property owned by Benjamin Barron.

The Wheeler greenhouses were built in 1890 and expanded in 1892. Rust-free asparagus is the crop for which the farm is best remembered. Other specialty crops raised on the farm were rhubarb and cucumbers. Esther Howe Anderson, daughter of Frank Wheeler, ran a truck farm on this acreage in the 1920s.

The Concord Free Public Library building, the gift of William Munroe, opened in 1873 with ten thousand books. It has been renovated from time to time to accommodate the growing book collection. Its archival collection preserves the town's rich historic past, and the fine art collection reinforces the significance of the town's famous men and women.

The West Concord School, built in 1897 on Church Street, was torn down sometime after the Harvey Wheeler School opened in 1918. Students could walk from one school to the other by way of a little path out the back door of the building shown here.

The Fowler Library was named for the postmaster, Loring Fowler, whose bequest enabled his daughter to commission a library for the people of West Concord. It was designed by Harry Little in 1930. He thoughtfully left room for expansion on the adjoining lot.

The cornerstone of the Episcopal chapel on Elm Street was laid in May 1883; the building (consecrated the following January) was designed by Concord's resident architect, John Chapman. Bronson Alcott donated $100 to the building fund. Additions were made in 1913, 1941 (design by Harry Little), 1948, and 1963 (design by Pietro Belluschi).

The Antiquarian Society (incorporated 1887) was created to accommodate the collection of antiquities gathered by Cummings Davis. Rooms in the Reuben Brown house on Lexington Road, and later at the junction of Lexington Road and Cambridge Turnpike, were decorated to display furniture and china in natural settings.

The West Concord Union Church was built in 1894. The "union" was between the Westvale group, the Reformatory group, and the group that met in Warner Hall. The church bell was donated in equal shares by Postmaster Loring Fowler and the Junction Reading Society. The sanctuary was remodeled in 1909 and again in 1985.

Daniel Chester French's studio (1879) was the location on October 25, 1895, for a meeting to celebrate the life of Thoreau. Some say it was the first meeting of the Thoreau Society. Besides Mrs. Kate Tryon (who was living there) and Alfred Hosmer, Franklin Sanborn, George Bartlett, Jane Hosmer, and Walton Ricketson were also present.

The Armory was built at 51 Walden Street in 1887 on property owned by Samuel Hoar for Company I, Sixth Regiment. The building became the home of the Concord Players in 1919. Their stage was designed by Clarence Blackall (father of Marian Blackall Miller), who designed (among many other things) the Colonial and Globe Theaters in Boston.

May Alcott was born in July 1840 in the Dovecote Cottage. She studied art and illustrated some of her sister's books, and she encouraged Daniel Chester French to become a sculptor. Her sketch of the Wayside is included in her book of collected drawings entitled *Concord Sketches*. She died in December 1879.

The Nashawtuc Reservoir was built in 1883 by William Wheeler. It supplemented the water supply brought from Sandy Pond in Lincoln. Its pipes ran along the causeway to West Concord and the Reformatory. The gatehouse was designed by John Chapman, who also designed Trinity Church Chapel.

The Franklin Sanborn house (1880) on Elm Street, next to the bridge, is a landmark at the foot of Nashawtuc Hill along the Sudbury River. Sanborn put love letters from his first wife, Ariana, into the west chimney. She died eight days after the wedding. His biography of Thoreau was published after he moved into the house.

The Dovecote Cottage was the first house the Alcott family lived in when they came to Concord in 1840. Louisa May Alcott wrote her first poem while living here. Also known as the Hosmer house, it was considered an old house in 1740. It was rebuilt in its present form in 1820.

Three

Recreation and Celebrations

The North Bridge is the most visited and most frequently photographed historic site in Concord. According to George Bartlett's 1885 *Guide Book*, it was a "very picturesque" spot for boaters. On the west side of the river is the Minuteman statue; the monument to the embattled farmers and the grave of the British soldiers are located on the east side.

John Maynard Keyes (1863–1933) was the nephew of Judge John Shepard Keyes. He was the road commissioner from 1901 to 1927 and also served on the Board of Selectmen. His interests were varied: antiques, real estate, an electric railroad, and a bicycle store on the Milldam. He enjoyed (and exploited) his resemblance to Theodore Roosevelt.

In the boating craze that captured Concord's enthusiasm in the 1880s, sailing canoes on the Concord River were not uncommon. This one, displayed by Henry Smith Jr. and Farnham Smith in their father's yard on Main Street, was typical of the type with sails low enough to fit underneath the bridges.

Dr. Edward Waldo Emerson often rode for pleasure on Concord's extensive woodland bridle paths. His favorite horse was named Roland. Dr. Emerson trained the horse and took particular pains to protect him from the discomforts of poor weather. When Roland had to be put down, Emerson performed the grim duty himself.

To

F. Hosford, Gen'l Man. B & L R.R.

We citizens of Concord respectfully and urgently remind you that your contractors are now building the new line through what is to us and to all lovers of nature most precious ground.

The No. Branch of Concord river is our "Central Park," and one of the most beautiful pieces of simple scenery in New England. We feel it is bad enough to have a railroad at all in that place, but the ruthless destruction of a single tree, or shrub, for fire wood or for any purpose not absolutely necessary to building the road will be viewed by us all as barbarism which we hope you can and will prevent.

Names	Names
R. Waldo Emerson	C. E. Barrett
A. Bronson Alcott	Elizabeth B. Ripley
F. B. Sanborn	Ann S. Brewster

The Middlesex Central Railroad plotted its course from Concord westward through the beloved grove of hemlocks along the Assabet River. This petition to save the trees was signed by Concord's most illustrious citizens. It was unsuccessful. The original document is in the Concord Library archives.

Charles H. Everett

E. K. S. Williams

E. J. Bartlett

Chas C. Brown

Frank Moore

J. W. Gilmore

F. H. Ellis

S. R. Bartlett

Geo E. Houghton

Alfred Munroe

Alfred W. Hosmer

Henry F. Brown

H. L. Whitcomb

William Le Brun

Jas W. Cutler

Wm H. Benjamin

J. H. Smith

Henry L. Damon

Charles W. Benjamin

E. P. Lathrop

Edward E. Rankin

N. B. Frith M.D.

Rob Chester Barrop

Annie C. Damon

Fannie C. Willis

S. H. Hurlbert

E. M. Smith

Grace W. Munns

E. B. Bartlett

Mary Hunt

Clara L. Hoar

Mrs Edward S. Hoar

Florence Hoar

E. S. Hoar

A. K. Bartlett

Caroline Hoar

F. H. Prichard

A. M. Prichard

Aline Reynolds

Louise Sommers

Fanny L. Sommers

Helen W. Blanchard

Caroline W. Perry

E. F. Smith

Hawthorne described the renowned hemlock trees on the Assabet River as having "outstretched arms as if resolute to take the plunge." It was a special spot for boaters. Many trees, destroyed to make way for the Middlesex Central Railroad in the 1870s, were replaced with willows.

Ralph "Peanut" Macone advertised his bicycle shop on Main Street with cheerful candor: "My shop is small and so am I. Why not give my goods a try." The business moved off the Milldam to larger quarters and flourished until the 1970s. Besides bicycles, the Macones sold other sporting goods, games, and toys.

When the town was first settled, according to Lemuel Shattuck, Concord's first historian, fish were abundant in the rivers: "salmon, shad, alewives, pike (pickerel) and dace . . . and some others." Fishing on the Assabet River was a favorite pastime in the nineteenth century. Now fishing is not permitted because of mercury pollution.

The Punkatasset Camp Fire Girls (1914) display honor beads indicating their achievements. The Camp Fire Girls organization (founded in 1910 by Mr. and Mrs. Luther Gulick) still serves girls of all races, nationalities, and creeds. In 1960, a U.S. postage stamp commemorated the Camp Fire Girls' fiftieth anniversary.

Skating on the meadows in 1886, very much a boy's sport until the 1870s, was only one of the recreational activities that year; tobogganing was the new fad. Occasionally the meadows froze sufficiently for excellent skating, sometimes even as far as Billerica, but the many ponds around Concord also provided fine opportunities.

Priscilla, a comic opera written by Henry D. Saltonstall and with music composed by T.W. Surette, was performed in the Concord Town Hall in March 1889. John Chapman, Concord's distinguished architect, was Hatebad Higgins (agent of the good ship Mayflower). A wax recording was made of the most memorable tunes from the show.

Literary clubs were very popular in Concord in the late 1800s. The first Shakespeare Club was started in 1871. The second Shakespeare Club (1878) held its meetings in the Association Hall over the post office in West Concord; in summer they shared literary papers and read poems at picnic meetings.

Croquet in 1882 was played within a specific playing area with four markers: at the starting point; at a circle six feet from the start; at the center; and at the goal (a board with arches equidistant from a peg over which was a white circle the same size as the ball). The object was to hit the goal circle without going through the arches or outside the boundaries.

The Social Circle describes itself: "without even the cohesion of a corporate existence, with no secrets or passwords or high-sounding titles, with only the ties of neighborhood and friendliness, and a common interest in the welfare of each other and of the town, it has been a noticeable part of the life and history of Concord."

Mary and Eliza Munroe kept house for their brother Alfred at his home at Main Street on the corner of Academy Lane, where William Lloyd Garrison, Wendell Phillips, and John Brown had been guests early in the nineteenth century. While the ladies enjoyed gardening as a pastime, Alfred played whist with his friends.

Edwin and Mary (Rice) Wheeler celebrated their golden wedding anniversary in 1895 with their six sons Elbert, Edwin, William, Frank, Harvey, and Sam. There were also two daughters: Eirene and Mary, who was an accomplished artist, owner of an electric car, and a friend of photographer Alfred Hosmer.

Harriet Lothrop (1844–1924), known as Margaret Sidney, is seen here enjoying the river with her daughter Margaret (the first child in one hundred years born at Wayside). Mrs. Lothrop wrote the *Little Peppers* series. She and her husband Daniel were not related to the Lathrops, daughter and son-in-law of Nathaniel Hawthorne, from whom they bought Wayside.

Golfers established a club in 1895 and built a course below Nashawtuc Hill under the supervision of William Wheeler. The grounds were prepared with a steam roller borrowed from the state. In 1897 a clubhouse was added for the pleasure and convenience of the players. The competitions were serious events entered with stern concentration and spirited resolve.

Nineteenth-century amusement facilities at Walden Pond included excursion boats, dining and dancing halls, a small zoo, swings, and bathhouses that went over the water so one could enter the water in privacy. An early public use of the pond was to celebrate emancipation of the slaves in the British West Indies.

Frogging on the Sudbury River on a July afternoon in 1931 was a pleasant pastime for boys who grew up on the river and knew its ways. Usually the frogs were used for bait. Other species along the muddy shore were fresh water clams, turtles (including bad-tempered snappers), and an occasional water snake.

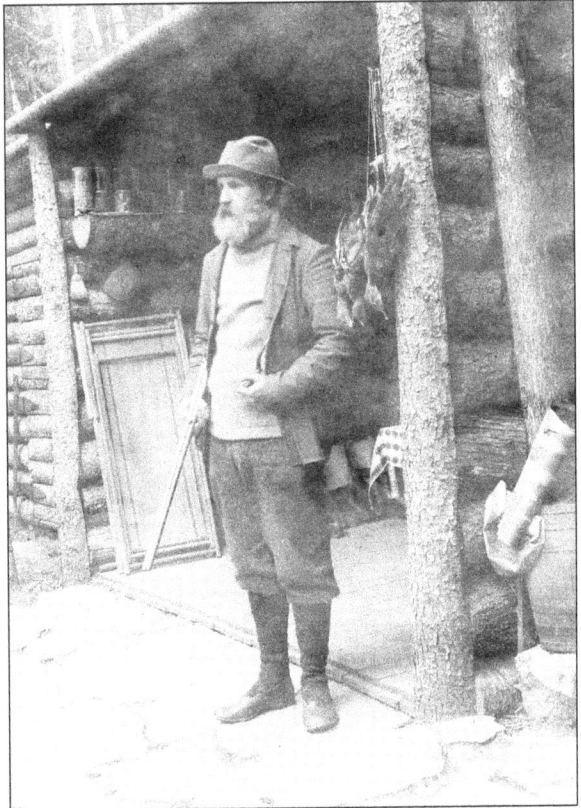

William Brewster (1851–1936), founder of the Nuttall Ornithological Club and first president of the Massachusetts Audubon Society, wrote descriptions of birds and animals that are models of careful observation, affection, and realistic sympathy. His close friend, Daniel Chester French, often accompanied him on his excursions on the river.

The Fairground at the end of Belknap Street, built in 1869, was the site of meets and races in 1895 under the aegis of the Concord Athletic Association. In addition to the rallies, the

Athletic Association sponsored horse-trotting competitions. The fastest time is said to have been 2.2450.

Bicycle racing was the favorite sport in the late 1890s. Bicycles were even sold at the local clothing store. There was a club in West Concord organized like a military company (complete with a captain and a bugler). On April 19, 1896, four thousand bicyclists arrived in Concord to enjoy the parade.

Hayriders bound for a picnic on Fairhaven Hill overlooking the river would have had a fine view of Walden Pond nearby, and a distant view of Mt. Wachuset and maybe even Mt. Monadnock. In 1880 there was a pine tree shrouding a niche in the cliffs known to romantic picnickers as the Retreat of Friendship.

Bunthorne is a character in Gilbert and Sullivan's operetta, *Patience*, which was performed numerous times in the Concord area in the early 1880s. It is probable that this group calling itself the Bunthorners was associated with those productions. The stars were William Barrett and John Chapman.

Tennis was the sport of choice in 1882, and within a year, a thirty-member club was formed to compete in the tournament held annually on Martha's Vineyard. Both men and women participated. There were badminton clubs, as well as tennis clubs, with competitions held for both men and women.

Baseball came to Concord in 1876, but it wasn't until 1889 that a team was formed at the high school. It was the first organized sport in the schools. By 1888 the Concord-Lexington game attracted twelve hundred spectators. Young men's groups, including the Knights of Columbus, played their games at the fairgrounds on Belknap Street.

Hammocks were common in Concord's backyards in the 1880s. Although Alfred Hosmer is best known for his photographs of Concord vistas, he is also remembered for his sensitive outdoor settings for children's portraits. Here are Maidie Brooks, daughter of George M. Brooks, and Richard Barrett. Both were born in 1877.

86

The centennial celebration in 1875 was a gala event. President Grant attended. In spite of the weather (20°), a near catastrophe (the grandstand collapsed), and the rage of Concord women (seats had not been saved for them), the day was proclaimed a success. The outdoor banquet for thousands has not been equaled by anything since. Emerson's oration included the following tribute to the Minutemen: "We have no need to magnify the facts . . . Only two of our men were killed at the bridge, and four others wounded."

The Melvin Memorial in Sleepy Hollow Cemetery was dedicated on June 16, 1909, the anniversary of the charge at Petersburg where one of the three Melvin boys was killed. Eighty-

eight members of the First Massachusetts Heavy Artillery came to dedicate the large marble memorial created by Daniel Chester French.

The celebration on Decoration Day in 1885 at Monument Square was organized by Sunday school teachers and their pupils. Graves of soldiers and town monuments were decorated. Townspeople contributed the flowers. Veterans were given a special invitation to participate in the ceremonies.

The 1930 celebration marking the incorporation of the town included a reenactment of Lafayette's visit to Concord in 1824. A reception was held at the Wright Tavern and was followed by dancing on the Church Green. Members of the Concord Players, (from left to right) Hans Miller, Fred Childs, and Herbert Hosmer, dressed up as Lafayette's son, Lafayette, and the secretary.

Eight-year-old William A. Buttrick (a descendent of Maj. John Buttrick who fought on April 19, 1775) was not too young to own a bicycle. He grew up to be a member of Concord's Board of Selectmen and the head of the Municipal Light Board. A widely respected member of the Concord community, he died in 1947.

The sesquicentennial celebration of the April 19 battle began at dawn with the 150 gun salute fired from Nashawtuc Hill. The parade included the display of eighty-nine Legion Post flags, some of which are shown here. The Marine band had to play in the Veterans Building because of bad weather. Fireworks and a ball completed the day.

At the Christmas Eve carol service at the First Parish Church in 1937, the minister read the Gospel of St. Luke, and the choir sang carols from others countries. *The Christmas Fanfare* scored for chorus and organ was written by Martin Shaw. The usual carol singing around the Monument Square tree was led by Arthur Lamb.

Exactly one year after their church burned on October 4, 1925, Trinitarians gathered together to lay the new cornerstone. The rash of fires in Concord suggested that the church fire was set. The identity of the arsonist was widely suspected, but no charges were ever brought against him.

The celebration marking the dedication of the Concord Boulder on Monument Square took place on May 25, 1924. Judge Prescott Keyes led the ceremony, and Rev. Benjamin Bulkeley read an original poem written especially for the ceremony. It concludes, "And when some mighty call is heard, / Reply as with a soldier's part."

Concord's high school band in 1940, under the direction of Mr. Enos Held, performed at both the New England Music Festival and the Massachusetts Music Festival. Their final performance was for the graduation ceremony at the State Armory. All senior members of the band received emblems.

Sleigh riding was an exciting family pastime in Concord as early as 1830. Each family used their own sleigh, and in a great gathering (sometimes as many as one hundred sleighs), they would go out the Union Turnpike and along the Groton Road to dine at a tavern in Littleton. Sometimes snow had to be piled onto the road to accommodate the sleighs.

94

Staples' Camp was a well-known camping place for ecologically minded men and women who loved the river. They sought to protect the river, its banks, and meadows from over use. Years later the camp became the home of Concord historian Ruth Wheeler. She died there in 1973. Of Staples, Thoreau wrote in 1857 that Staples "says he came to Concord some twenty-four years ago a poor boy with a dollar and three cents in his pocket, and he spent the three cents for drink at Bigelow's Tavern, and now he's worth 'twenty hundred dollars clear.' . . . I told him that he had done better than I in a pecuniary respect, for I had only earned my living."

The Jolly Ten were spirited young people of the town who found each other's company congenial. The group has evidently dressed up for an event of some importance. The women's hats are at the peak of fashion, possibly the creations of Miss Buck, a woman who specialized in ladies' finery.

Sam Hosmer, Danny Keyes, and John Eaton are pictured here from left to right on their bicycles in the 1935 tercentenary parade. They won third prize for their entry in the business group of the parade. Other entries included a lady in a giant hoop skirt, a replica of Thoreau's hut, and Dr. Sheehan impersonating Dr. Minot treating Minutemen.

In 1920 a piano in a parlor made a social statement. Piano playing, for soirées, singalongs, and informal recitals, was a common form of at-home recreation. Pictured here is the parlor of Harriet Clark, a music teacher in the Concord schools for forty-seven years. She died in 1933.

Town swimming lessons introduced many families to the pleasures of swimming at Walden Pond. The eastern end of the pond was designated as the swimming area, and floating rafts were used for diving. In earlier years, skinny dippers seeking privacy used the western side, but they were often surprised by tourists visiting the Thoreau cove and cairn site.

The flora along the Mill Brook has interested naturalists for more than a century. Where dandelions once grew in a meadow setting, there is now (according to a 1996 survey) a proliferation of red maples, buckthorn, five species of ferns, skunk cabbage, and loosestrife.

Four

Roadways, Rivers, and Streams

Three bridges carry the town's traffic out of town to points west. At one time, in addition to the railroad track, there was also a trolley track; automobiles and trucks crossed the river on the South Bridge (Route 62) as well as the Elm Street Bridge (Union Turnpike).

Crosby's Corner, now a major intersection on the east side of Concord, was rebuilt in the early 1930s as part of the construction of the new bypass section of Route Two, the western route

An army of cement trucks owned by B. Perini & Sons of Framingham was used to complete construction of the Concord bypass in record time. Fifteen miles of the new roadway between

from Cambridge to the Berkshires. The labor force was referred by the National Re-employment Service office, located in the old high school on Stow Street.

Alewife and the Concord Reformatory cost $2 million at the height of the Depression.

Walden Breezes, the trailer park and refreshment stand next to Walden Pond, has been a landmark (some say an eyesore) for more than sixty years. It was the setting for a mystery story by Jane Langton during controversy over the Concord dump that was located next to the trailer park.

Dredgers deepened the channel of the river to accommodate larger boats needed to move merchandise from the mills, building materials for construction, and "for restoration of marshes, abatement of malaria and other perils." The dredged mud was left in the meadows or in deeper parts of the river.

The bridge over the Assabet River by the Concord Reformatory was rebuilt at the time of the construction of the Concord bypass, and the new causeway made it possible to use the bridge in time of high water. Construction of this bridge, the railroad bridge at Route 62, and the railroad bridge at Walden Pond cost $70,000.

Derby's Bridge across the Assabet River on Main Street near the present intersection of Main Street and Baker Avenue was replaced in stone during 1886. The approaches were raised so the bridge could be crossed in time of high water. The costs were $6,400 for the bridge and $1,100 for the approaches.

The intersection at the Concord Reformatory—not a rotary—connected the bypass section of the new highway with the Mohawk Trail part of Route 2. The branch road leading to

The new bridge over the Sudbury River, built in the early 1930s as part of the Concord bypass, was the most expensive bridge of the bypass project. A 12-foot channel was dug for boat

West Concord appears on the left, and Route 2A is on the right. The main thoroughfare goes straight through.

traffic. Its construction wiped out the Clamshell Hill site of important Native American relics mentioned by Thoreau.

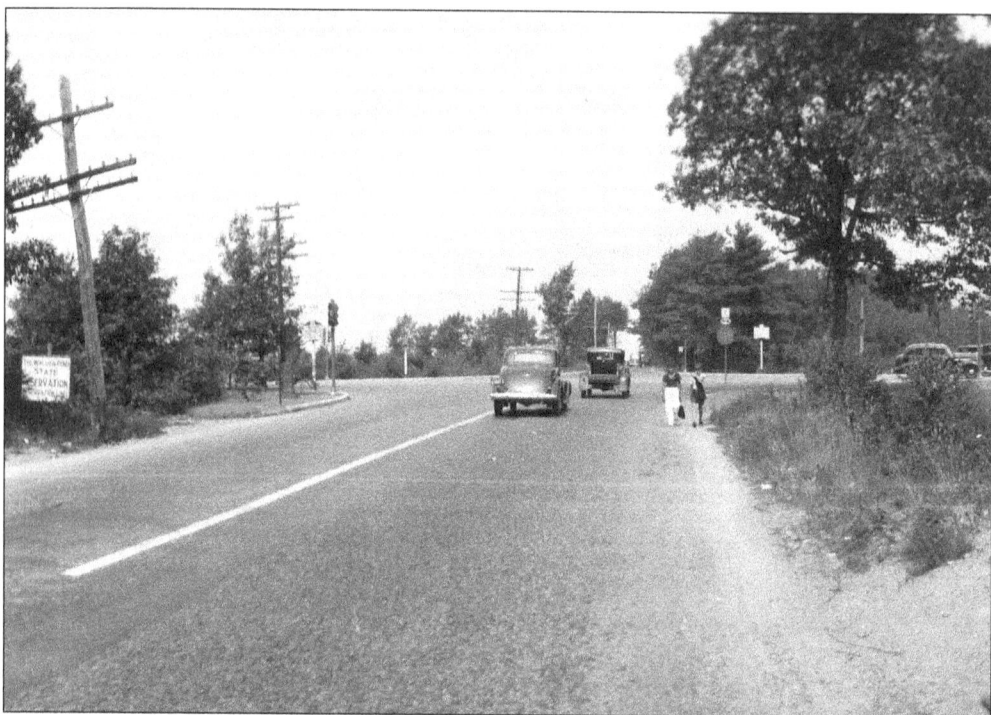

The intersection at Route 126 from Walden Pond into Concord was relocated to accommodate the bypass road. Waste ground was appropriated for the 100-foot right of way. Twenty-three percent of the $100,000 allotted land damage apportionment was designated for Concord.

The intersection of Walden and Thoreau Streets, with Fairyland on the left, was rebuilt at the time of the construction of the new bypass, and Brister's Hill Road was created. The road to

In order to connect the Cambridge Turnpike with the new bypass section at the foot of Lincoln hill—Crosby's Corner—considerable reconstruction was necessary. The swamp area was filled in, trees were cut down, and the old road was buried. An all-important stone crusher was located near this area.

the present high school can be seen on the right. These road construction jobs employed 118 Concord men.

The intersection of Walden and Hubbard Streets, first the location of the Ebenezer Hubbard house, then the George Brabrook house, is now the site of Concord's post office. Early

Fallen trees all over the town broke electric wires during the 1938 hurricane. In the aftermath of the devastating storm, a resourceful boy at the Minuteman Service Station connected his bicycle to the gas pump's pumping mechanism and made gas flow by pedaling hard and fast.

automobile travel through town is confirmed by a gas station where the livery had been located.

Before the days of mechanization, road construction was a laborious business. The roadbed had to be built up with layers of sand and stone so vehicles would not get stuck in the spring mud. Adding sand to the surface of the road was necessary as well, because it blew away and was worn off by the passing vehicles.

Watering trucks, with two sprinklers on the back, each with a capacity of about 700 gallons, were used to keep down the dust from the gravel roads. The town purchased a Studebaker Street Sprinkler (capacity 750 gallons) for $450 in 1894. It was a treat for small boys to get squirted by the sprinkler as it went by.

The blizzard on February 2, 1898, brought the town to a standstill. The plows couldn't keep up, and there was nowhere to put the huge amounts of snow. Main Street was completely filled with snow. The cost to the town for snow removal was remarked on for several years in the annual town reports.

The worst ice storm in thirty years, at the end of November 1921, was caused by a series of rain storms followed by freezing temperatures. Trees, bushes, and wires were brought down by the weight of the ice. The trolley couldn't run on the obstructed tracks. Curiously, just a few miles to the south of Concord, there was neither ice nor sleet.

The November 1921 ice storm damaged Concord's fine old elm trees and orchards. Power and telephone outages were widespread, but the mail got through because the trains could still run. The huge willow on Monument Street was badly broken. Sentimental townspeople hoped that the "old hero" would survive.

Cleaning up after the 1938 hurricane was a monumental job. An estimated twelve hundred trees were blown down by the vicious storm that struck after rainstorms had softened the ground and loosened the tree roots. One victim of the storm was the Monument Square elm—the whipping post tree—in front of the Town House.

The Cambridge Turnpike (Lincoln Road) bridge has always been a headache for road crews. The Mill Brook wetlands between Hawthorne Lane and Lexington Road (Bay Road) and the wetlands between the road and the town forest are close to the level of the road so there is little leeway for overflow.

The Concord, Maynard and Hudson trolley ran for close to twenty years, for 20¢ (round trip), on a 15-mile route that took an hour and fifteen minutes. Excursion cars had wicker chairs, card tables, colored lights, and carpets. More than 52,000 patrons used the line in the second month of operation.

Warner's Pond is named for Ralph Warner. He developed the part of West Concord around the prison. In the late nineteenth century the pond was a much frequented recreation spot, with ice houses and camps along the shore; there was even a touring boat, the *Maude Blake*, that circulated around the tiny islands.

The 1936 flood did more damage in the center of Concord than at other locations around town primarily because the Mill Brook culvert under the road was inadequate, so water backed

Anderson's store was particularly badly affected by the 1936 flood. The National Guard was called out (the townspeople, directed by Gladys Hosmer, served them corn chowder). A young

up into the stores' basements. The firemen worked overtime trying to keep merchandise from getting soaked.

man in a fur coat fell into the brook as it rushed beneath the stores. He was rescued, but his fur coat was ruined.

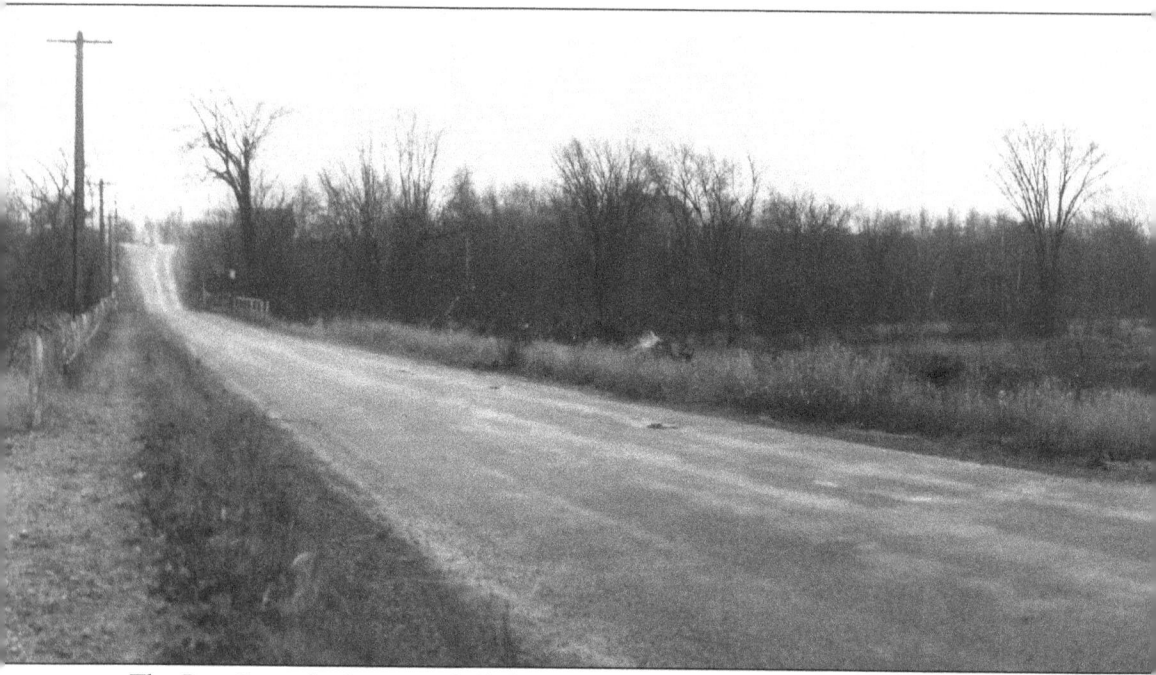

The Pine Street bridge was, of all the bridges in Concord, the one most in danger of being washed out by the flood of 1936. It was the only wooden pile bridge in town, and 100 feet of

During the 1936 flood, the Minuteman statue was rumored to be threatened by the flood waters. Tourists flocked to the North Bridge to see the high water, but the statue was never in danger.

roadway by the bridge was under water. Sandbags and pumps saved it. The causeway has since been raised.

The bridge, however, took a considerable beating. Extensive repairs to the underpinnings were necessary after the water went down.

The present South Bridge boathouse is located on the site of the boathouse used by the Garland School on Wood Street in the 1880s. The Canoe Club boathouse was much nearer the North

The Liberty Street and Lowell Road intersection was one of those you-can't-get-there-from-here spots in Concord during the 1936 flood, even though extensive work had been done in

Bridge. Nowadays South Bridge canoes are rented all summer, and a restaurant boat takes passengers for a luncheon sail down the river.

previous years to ensure access to the Red Bridge. Filling the approaches was welcome winter employment for the men and exercise for horses.

Fairyland Pond in the Hapgood Wright Town Forest is a short distance from Goose Pond and Walden Pond, but the distance seems greater since the bypass has separated the smaller pond

In 1895 George Bartlett's friends made an illustrated autograph book celebrating their visits to Bartlett's boathouse behind the Old Manse. The canoes stored here were designed by Walton Ricketson, son of Thoreau's friend Daniel Ricketson; they were constructed by Concord's most famous canoe builder, George Warren.

from its southern relatives. Creation of the pond changed the height of the water table in the surrounding area.

A muddy road in spring was a common occurrence in Concord. Some thought the excessive number of shade trees kept dampness in the ground. Whatever it was, the road commissioners declared that proper management of the roadways could not be assured if it was left to the "choice, caprice or selfish indifference" of the towns.

The flooded meadows below Nashawtuc Hill are an important part of the river's natural flood control system. They provide hay for cattle in summer and skating for the townspeople in winter. The Native American name for the meadow land was *moskeht* (grass) and *ohkeit* (ground), which English tongues pronounced *Musketaquid.*

The promontory on the Sudbury River, downstream from Lee's Bridge, was named Martha's Point for George Bartlett's sister, "a lady of literary taste and culture." According to the naturalist Richard Eaton, in the nineteenth century the rock was "subjected to wear and tear by ever-increasing numbers of undiscriminating visitors."

The Great Meadows lie along the Concord River, about a mile from Concord Center. The dikes, completed in 1929, are used extensively by bird watchers and casual hikers. The ponds are often filled with flocks of mallard ducks and geese feeding on the wild rice. The area is now managed by the National Wildlife Refuge.

The Mill Brook rises in the Bedford flats, wends its way through the meadows between Lexington Road and Cambridge Turnpike, and then turns toward Concord Center. It runs through a culvert underneath the stores in the center of town and empties into the river just below the Red Bridge.

Goose Pond, Thoreau said, was a name used as early as 1653, but Channing, Thoreau, and Emerson, in admiration of the ripples on these two small ponds, called them Ripple Lakes. Channing wrote, "When the playful breeze drops on the pool it springs to right and left, quick as a kitten playing with dead leaves."

Andromeda Pond south of Walden Pond is really a string of small swampy areas. The terrain is easiest traversed in winter when ice makes "hummock jumping" less hazardous. Thoreau commented on the rose-colored ice "with internal bluish tinges like mother-o'-pearl or the inside of a conch."

Ice making was a highly profitable enterprise in Concord in the nineteenth century, particularly after the railroad became available to carry the ice into Boston and points south. Angier's Pond made a fine source for ice, and Walden and Warner's Ponds were extensively cut.

White Pond's water is as spectacularly clear as the water at Walden Pond. Channing wrote, "I love Thy gleams, White Pond! thy dark, familiar grove; Thy deep green shadows, clefts of pasture ground; mayhap a distant bleat the single sound." Now, the pond is a private swimming area for Concord families.

Hiram W. Blaisdell's map was made in 1875. Mr. Blaisdell was born in Concord and graduated from MIT with a degree in engineering. He belonged to the Concord Dramatic Club and served as a stage manager in their productions. He later moved out West and ultimately settled in Pennsylvania.

Fairhaven Bay (70 acres) is an enlarged section of the Sudbury River between Lincoln and Concord, a centuries-old camping, picnicking, and fishing place below the Fairhaven Cliffs. It "lies more open and can be seen from more distant points than any of our ponds," Thoreau wrote in his *Journal* in 1852.

Gowing Swamp is really a quaking, sphagnum bog. Channing, probably thinking Hawthorne would like this strangely gothic marsh, took him to see it, but Hawthorne was not impressed. "Take me away from this stinking hole," he said. It was bought by the Sudbury Valley Trustees in 1970.

Walden Pond is still a place of inspiration for Thoreau pilgrims who come to visit the site of Thoreau's hut. But the pond is also used extensively by swimmers, sun bathers, boaters, hikers, picnickers, fishermen, and skaters, who carry on the century-old tradition of utilizing the pond as a recreational area.